MAKING SENSE OF BEHAVIOUR

LEARNING TO WAVE:

Some Everyday Guidelines

for Stress Management

by

Rob Long

A NASEN PUBLICATION

Published in 1999

ISBN 1 901485 12 9

Published by NASEN.
NASEN is a company limited by guarantee, registered in England and Wales. Company No. 2674379.
NASEN is a registered charity. Charity No. 1007023.

Further copies of this book and details of NASEN's many other publications may be obtained from the Publications Department at its registered office: NASEN House, 4/5 Amber Business Village, Amber Close, Amington, Tamworth, Staffs. B77 4RP.
Tel: 01827 311500; Fax: 01827 313005
Email: welcome@nasen.org.uk; Website: www.nasen.org.uk

Cover design by Raphael Creative Design.
Typeset in Times by J. C. Typesetting and printed in the United Kingdom by Stowes (Stoke-on-Trent).

Contents

Preface

Learning to Wave: Some Everyday Guidelines for Stress Management is one of eight booklets in the series *Making Sense of Behaviour* by Rob Long. The others are *Exercising Self-control; Developing Self-esteem through Positive Entrapment for Pupils facing Emotional and Behavioural Difficulties; Friendships; Understanding and Supporting Depressed Children and Young People; Not Me, Miss! The Truth about Children who Lie; Supporting Pupils with Emotional and Behavioural Difficulties through Consistency;* and *Challenging Confrontation: Information and Techniques for School Staff.*

Learning to Wave is written for teachers themselves. It contains advice about coping with the stress which might arise from dealing with children with behavioural problems. *Challenging Confrontation* gives information and techniques for teachers to use when dealing with argumentative, angry and difficult pupils and *Supporting Pupils with Emotional and Behavioural Difficulties through Consistency* advocates a whole-school approach for low-level misbehaviours.

The other five titles give practical ideas and information for teachers to use with children with worrying behaviours in their classes. These are written to help teachers both understand and change some of the difficulties that children might experience (depression, lack of self-control, low self-esteem, friendship problems and lying).

Each book stands alone but when read as a set the behavioural issues and their solutions overlap and this emphasises the need for positive and consistent strategies to be put into place throughout the school.

Acknowledgements
The author and publishers wish to express their grateful thanks to Lorna Johnston, Agnes Donnelly and Dorothy Smith for their helpful suggestions and comments.

Learning to Wave:
Some Everyday Guidelines for Stress Management

Introduction

There are times when life seems to go from bad to worse, such as when going to work becomes part of the problem, and perhaps home life is not as great as it could be. Teachers and support staff know what pressure is about.

- How often are new targets set before you've completed the previous ones?
- How often do pupils bruise your shins and tell you to **** ***?
- How often do you wish for a change in career?

The constant change which seems to be forever taking place and the challenging and troubled behaviour of more and more children add to the pressure. The list goes on and on. Much has been written about managing stress. This booklet is intended to be a brief but meaningful reminder as to what teachers and support staff can do for themselves. We all agree that schools and the education system need to recognise and support the ever-growing numbers who are affected by stress/ill health to the point of wishing to leave the profession. "Learning to Wave" aims to remind teachers and support staff that they need to look after themselves more than ever. To be a "chalk face warrior" requires a positive attitude about self-care. Who else is going to care for you or understand you if you don't? The emphasis here will be more on what to do about stress rather than the theory of it. There are many useful books and courses that can help individuals do more to prevent those everyday pressures becoming serious stressors; "Learning to Wave" is a quick, personal M.O.T.

As you read this you will be expected to carry out numerous activities. Whether or not you do will always be your choice. You know that the fact that you are prepared to read this suggests that you probably think things could be better. Make the right choice, read on and begin to plan for change. Throughout, I have used the term "feeling" as a commonly used equivalent of the term "emotion".

Accept
Imagine you are driving your car in an area that you know well. You don't need a map. You know where there are potholes to avoid, one-way streets etc. Even when you do get lost there is no need to worry, you know who to ask, or phone. You know the rules.

YOU ARE IN CONTROL

Now imagine that one day you find yourself in a new and unknown area. You realise that you don't understand the signs. Drivers behave very differently. Your previous knowledge and understanding no longer apply. The rules are different here.

YOU ARE OUT OF CONTROL

This is similar to what happens when stress takes control. You are used to being in an "emotional world" where positive emotions rule. You are used to success. You feel in control, your world is mapped out. You are good to people and they to you. The emotions that dominate are those involved with joy, happiness, love etc.

BUT we all sometimes visit a different emotional landscape. This may be through bereavement or family breakup, or pressures at work. Under such circumstances we experience natural emotions such as anger, loss and despair. We are less familiar with this world. We do not know if what we are feeling is normal. The emotions affect both our thoughts and behaviour. We are frightened. We have no map. We may question our sanity.

Understanding emotions

If we did not have emotions we would have no problems and no fun. Data, in Star Trek, is neither happy nor sad. Emotions give our lives colour and meaning. They also help us learn. Events that threaten us make us frightened and we are more likely to remember the event and learn to avoid it. Our emotions were invaluable for our ancestors who lived in the jungle. They helped us survive. It makes good sense if a tiger attacks that you learn very quickly to avoid tigers. Emotions put the zip into such learning. This is "one trial learning". But we no longer live or work in the jungle. (Sometimes it just feels like it!)

Emotions do not follow rational rules, so we are often caught out by them. We try to think in a rational, logical way. Emotions are neither rational nor irrational. Because we are unfamiliar with their rules we are vulnerable to their powers. When we are surrounded by positive ones we manage well. But when we get drawn into the land of negative emotions we are at risk.

Emotional principles
1. Emotions can be changed indirectly not directly.
2. Painful emotions can be part of a natural healing process.
3. Emotions encourage thoughts and actions which help them persist.
4. The more a negative emotion is avoided the stronger its influence is.
   (These principles are expanded on the next page.)

When we have more pressures than we can cope with we are threatened. Emotions warn us about the danger through switching on the "flight or fight" response. Our bodies become tense and ready for action. Our emotions become negative through fear and threat of attack. We have arrived in a world which we are unprepared for. The pressures increase, our thoughts become more negative, our behaviour more erratic, aggressive etc. We have arrived. We are trapped. We drive around in circles. Our behaviour pushes people away from us. (Rejection feeds our anger.) We can only see the problems that face us. (Negativity feeds depression.) We care less for our looks. (Neglect feeds our isolation and loneliness.) Can you see how your thoughts, behaviours and feelings all tend to support each other?

You have arrived. You are in danger of becoming trapped in a world where the signposts are for:

- negativity
- futility
- isolation
- depression
- pointlessness
- anger
- sadness
- cynicism
- worthlessness

An example of this internal logic for negative emotions is depression. Depression gets us into a hole and keeps us digging. It wants us to see the bad side of things, to see problems all the time, not to care about our appearances, not to smile. All of these are the "right" ways to behave to enable the depression to continue to be fed. It doesn't want us to climb out of the hole. That would be the end of it.

Remember in schools we are under pressures which lead us to act in ways which can be less than positive or in our best interests. For you to be able to continue each week and reach the end of a term able to benefit from the holidays you will need to make some serious decisions.

Start now, sign up.

I ACCEPT THAT I AM A LEARNER DRIVER IN A LAND WHOSE TRAFFIC RULES I DO NOT FULLY UNDERSTAND. (I ONLY INTENDED A BRIEF VISIT.) I WILL NEED TO LEARN OR PRACTISE THESE SKILLS TO ENABLE ME TO RETURN TO MY HOME COUNTRY.

Signed .... Date ....

Key principles

As we increase our understanding of emotions we are learning key principles. The more we understand these then the better able we will be to take control and influence them in a positive way. Without this understanding you will remain a victim to them.

1. Emotions can be changed indirectly not directly

This means that we can influence how we feel by what we think and what we do. We have direct, voluntary control over each of these. Therefore these two can be used to help change our emotions.

2. Painful emotions can be part of a natural healing process

When we are hurt there are natural emotions that need to be expressed if we are to come to terms with the experience.

3. Adults can work hard to avoid the very emotions they most need

An adult who seems very defensive and distant is most in need of friendship, care and support.

4. Emotions encourage thoughts and actions which help them persist

Emotions have an internal logic which seeks to maintain their existence. For example, depression will encourage negative thinking, anger will support aggressive behaviour, anxiety will seek uncertainty, and love will seek to belong.

5. Negative emotions hinder learning

When controlled by strong negative emotions such as fear, anger and depression, learning new skills becomes more difficult.

6. The more a negative emotion is avoided the stronger its influence is

When we try to avoid painful emotions we need to use more and more energy through employing defence mechanisms to keep guard against the emotion breaking through into consciousness.

7. There are natural emotions associated with having. These include joy, love, hope, interest and curiosity and emotions associated with loss, anger, jealousy, fear and sorrow

There are emotions we naturally experience in positive relationships, or when we achieve goals or meet new challenges etc. There are also emotions we experience when we lose someone or something we love and care for. These are healing emotions. When anger turns to hatred, fear to avoidance and jealousy to possessiveness then the emotion is no longer positive.

8. Emotions are psychological experiences

Emotions are neither rational nor irrational, they happen in response to events. They are not governed by the same principles as thoughts.

The Plan - Thoughts, Feelings and Actions

You have perhaps already noticed that there are three core aspects involved. These are Thoughts, Feelings and Actions.

The figure on the following page shows that each of these affects others and is affected by them in turn. Therefore if you think negative thoughts then you will feel low and act in a negative manner. It all makes simple sense. The more you think those thoughts the stronger they become. This is like furrowing a thinking rut through your mind. Now each time you need to think it's usually negative. We have already said that we cannot directly change what we feel. Otherwise we would just "snap out of it". But we can take control of what we think and what we do. It might not be easy at first. But then making the choice to change is in itself part of the solution.

9

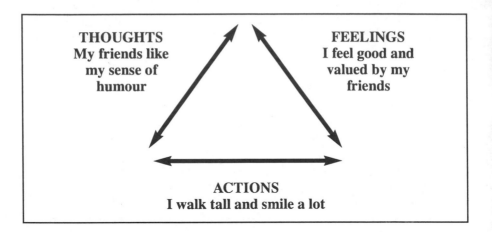

THOUGHTS
My friends like
my sense of
humour

FEELINGS
I feel good and
valued by my
friends

ACTIONS
I walk tall and smile a lot

We will now look at ideas for taking control of our thoughts and actions. There is no "quick fix" solution. When you become a victim of negative pressure it is not your fault. You need to now start climbing out of the hole. Nobody else will or can do it for you. You are worth it. All of your negative reactions are part of the problem and should not therefore be listened to. If you had mumps, and the mumps could talk, would they want to be got rid of? Your negative thoughts are not you. They are part of the stress you are experiencing. Imagine you take your mumps to the doctors. The doctors prescribe certain medication. Do you argue about taking it? You are about to be shown what are the right things for you to do with your thoughts and actions. You are not being asked to agree with them or not. Your task is to choose those that will help. Many of them you will already be doing.

Thoughts
How can we take control of our thoughts? Well, we can begin by recognising that while we have thoughts, we are more than our thoughts. I can choose to think about my holiday last year, or the tasks I have yet to complete today. We are more than our thoughts. The more we allow our negative thoughts time, the more we energise/charge them up. When we turn to our more positive thoughts we find them weak, shrivelled and only half complete. We must learn positive statements about ourselves and use them on a regular basis.

CHOOSE FIVE STATEMENTS FROM THE LIST ON PAGE 18 AND
LEARN THEM. REHEARSE THEM AT SET TIMES EACH DAY.
WHEN YOU KNOW THEM WELL TRY A NEW FIVE.

If you are plagued by negative thoughts then try these tricks. First wear an elastic band on your wrist and whenever you find yourself thinking negatively, flick it and change to different thoughts. Have a very special thought ready to switch to.

Allow yourself five minutes each day when you will allow all these negative thoughts a chance to run around. But only then and only for five minutes.

Let's imagine that you could drive around inside my thoughts and that you take a wrong turning and find yourself in my "dark lands". This is where the emotions are negative and all thoughts associated with them are equally black and despairing. Can you see that to help me find my way back whenever I go there, I have tried to put up signposts? (Just as when I fall into depression, I have learned to leave the shovel behind and start climbing up the foot holes I have left during previous visits.)

In my mind map, the markers are especially relevant to me. You will have to create your own. Mine are markers that let me know that "the edge is near, say 500 metres away". Or "Proceed with Caution Falling Rocks". In reality my markers say things like this:

- Is this a problem or just an inconvenience?
- If it is the right thing to do - do it.
- Look for solutions not problems.
- Happiness cannot be pursued, it ensues from doing.
- Life is asking you for meaning. Live with style.
- Don't ask "Why me?", ask "Why not me?"
- When the pupil is ready the teacher will appear.
- Life is offering support, be ready to receive it.

Now each of these has especial relevance for me. I'm sure you can think of your own. Can you see that when I am drawn into my negative side I am trying to make sure I know my way back? They are my markers. As you look around you can see that I have planted positive thoughts even in this darkness. It takes time, but the very effort is rewarding in itself. Try and see if it helps you. If not, leave it behind.

If you are plagued by unwanted thoughts, try confronting them completely. Often such thoughts have power because we use mental energy to avoid them. It's like the scratching at the window in the middle of the night. It can be really scary until you look and find it's a leaf. Imagine the worst. What would happen? Would you survive? The answer will be yes. Take the emotional power from these thoughts and face them. "I can cope with that."

If you have some really weird and frightening thoughts at times (welcome to the human race), then associate them with something really bizarre. So that every time they appear in your mind they have the silly event with them to remind you that these are just irrational thoughts. Do not take them seriously. They are not worth it. I have some thoughts that I have now associated with the sound of an African Funk Band. Every time these thoughts get triggered I can hear the whistles and the music starting up in the background. This reminds me of the kind of thoughts I am dealing with.

At the start of each day decide something you would like to accomplish. Make sure that you are setting small achievable goals. Work out what rewards you will treat yourself with for success. At the end of each day reflect on what you have achieved and look for any bonuses.

MASTER YOUR THINKING - HAVE A PLAN
DON'T GET CAUGHT WITH YOUR PLANS DOWNS

Feelings
While we are not able to directly change our emotions we can do a lot that can help us experience positive feelings. I see a lot of these ideas as being "mental health" vitamins. If we do a selection of these each day then we are doing the right things that will support. You can add a lot more that are unique to you. Include them. Your task will be to choose a minimum of three each day and to do them, each day.

- If you enjoy music make sure that you play a selection that lifts and inspires you.
- When you choose to read make sure that you have novels or whatever that are positive and lift your spirits.
- Walking on the coast or on open moor land can be very positive for the emotions as well as the body. (An old recreation for depression, cynicism etc was to recommend the person spent an hour at sunrise in a cemetery. This focuses the mind.)

- Clothes, hairdos, all of these are ways in which we can produce a more positive effect.
- Art, sculpture, each of these can work to create positive feelings.
- Humour. We should always try to ensure that we smile or laugh each day. Laughter is a very good form of exercise. It releases tension. Whatever it is that you find funny, don't hope for it, build it into your day.
- Have you ever noticed how good you feel when you help someone? This is a very positive way of lifting your emotions and somebody else's at the same time.
- Various pursuits such as painting, writing, poetry, patchworking, sewing, playing music can each help our emotions.
- Being with children and babies can help refocus our thoughts and feelings on to what really matters.
- Colours and smells around your house are a good way to create an environment that is supportive.
- Gardens can be a pleasure both to create and enjoy. Time taken in designing and developing will pay back ample emotional rewards.
- Food and wine can similarly give us enjoyments that should not be taken for granted.
- Traditional and New Age religions can give emotional value and spiritual meaning.

> EACH DAY WE NEED TO RECHARGE OURSELVES.
> DON'T JUST HOPE FOR A GOOD DAY - PLAN ONE.

If you have found it extremely difficult to choose any of the above activities then try the task on page 17. It is designed for you. It will involve you actively rating various activities that you engage in throughout the day to help you find what it is that you enjoy doing. You will then be ready to start rebuilding an emotional life. What has happened to you is that you have been switched onto negative, draining emotions for too long. You have lost the immediate ability to recognise the small pleasures in life. It happens. Change it, start now!

Body actions
When we are distressed our body is switched to red alert. It is ready to act - fight or flight. Because we do not use this energy we are likely to suffer

muscle tension and the like. The body is where the effects of prolonged stress will be readily seen. In the short term we will suffer headaches, rashes, more colds etc. But in the long run we are talking about ulcers, nervous breakdown and heart attacks. Our body is where we live. Some people spend more time and attention on their house than their own bodies. We all appreciate the need to watch what we eat, drink and smoke. We need to care for our body much more.

Exercise
We each need about 20 minutes of exercise each day. If you are not quite doing this yet, make a start. It might just be walking around the garden or to the local shop. Begin small, you're bound to succeed, and then you'll feel like doing more. We weren't all meant to be out jogging every night. Swimming, walking, cycling are all very good. You need a strong heart to teach.

Breathing
Practise calm controlled breathing. Breathe deeply and fill your diaphragm. Shallow breathing is inefficient and increases stress. The out breath is the important relaxation one. Make sure your posture is right. Bad posture adds to your discomfort. Avoid crossed legs, save your energy for what matters.

Relaxation
We all need to relax. Our muscles tense up through the day so make sure that you have a number of ways in which you unwind. We each have our favourite ways for doing this, page 12 gives you some ideas to explore. Your task is to find what is right for you and do them each and every day.

Sleeping
It is impossible to give your best if you've only slept for some three or four hours. To be in bed physically exhausted but mentally alert with the names of pupils or whatever going around in your head is helping no one. (Remember that if you have physical symptoms or want advice about sleeping a good G.P. is invaluable.) To achieve sleep when we are stressed will be difficult. But a plan of action can help. Design a routine and stick with it for some time. Establish what you feel is a good night-time routine. Consider the following, make your plan and do it! This is mine:

I am to:

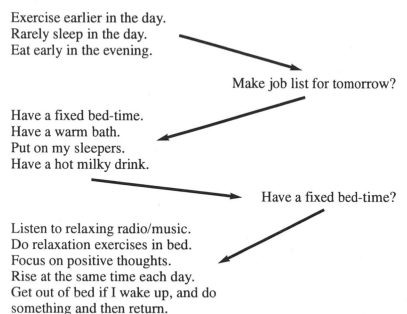

Exercise earlier in the day.
Rarely sleep in the day.
Eat early in the evening.

Make job list for tomorrow?

Have a fixed bed-time.
Have a warm bath.
Put on my sleepers.
Have a hot milky drink.

Have a fixed bed-time?

Listen to relaxing radio/music.
Do relaxation exercises in bed.
Focus on positive thoughts.
Rise at the same time each day.
Get out of bed if I wake up, and do
something and then return.

Night-time exercises for the mind

While it is essential to have a good bed-time routine there will be
times when this is just not enough. Now is the time to learn some Mind
Control activities. So if you're awake at 3:00 a.m. when everything is so
much worse, mainly because there is no way you can do anything about
anything, then join me in a few night-time activities. All in the mind, of
course!

This is not the time

Tell yourself that this is not the time. Keep a notebook by the bed so that
you can jot it down and deal with it in the morning.

Is this the worry?

There are two things that are not worth worrying about. Those that you can
do something about and those that you can't. Which is this?

Relaxation

Focus on your breathing and think and feel exactly what it is like as you
breathe in and out.

15

How many sheep?

See how many sheep (or whatever you fancy) you can count. Picture them passing through a narrow gate. If you wander off, or the sheep do, don't worry. Gently bring your mind back to the task at hand.

Backward numbers

Take a high number and count slowly backwards. Count one number for each breath. If you get distracted reset yourself and start again.

Countdown

Imagine somewhere where you were calm and relaxed. Picture all the details. Now imagine a stairway with ten steps leading down to it. At each step feel yourself feeling calmer and more relaxed. When you arrive there just focus on all the good feelings you have. Do not worry about sleeping, enjoy where you are.

Counting games are good because they are simple and monotonous, they need little effort. They just divert your mind from the thinking about other things. As you start to tire, you may well find the worries return. Accept this as it happens and gently pull your mind back to the activity.

Time passes

Imagine watching the second hand of a clock slowing down and finally stopping.

Alternative tasks

If you cannot get to sleep or you wake up have a number of set activities to do. These should be in another room and should be unstimulating, ideally something that you place very low priority on such as a monotonous activity, eg sorting buttons into colours and sizes, or whatever. (It must be something that you're not going to look forward to finishing off the following night.)

Repeat sleep facts

Evidence suggests that 65% of people sleep between 6.5 and 8.5 hours each night. A few people are fine on 4 hours while a few need 10. We all need less sleep as we get older and wiser. Sleep happens in cycles; it is common to wake when we are in a light sleep and then to return to a deeper sleep. An hour of sleep before midnight is worth, yes you've guessed, the same as an hour of sleep at any other time. A change in sleep pattern will take several weeks to take effect.

Occasional poor nights will not affect your work performance the next day.

Exercises

Accentuating the Positive

1. Note what you are doing, on the hour throughout the day and how you feel about what you are doing. Score how you felt on a scale of 0 = the worst you could feel, to 9 = the best you could feel. Put the scores into the attached record sheet.
2. At the end of the first day find your average score. Then look back through the days and using a highlighter mark all scores that were above the average.
3. Put a P for pleasure if the increased score was on account of Pleasure, when something nice happened to you or when you did something enjoyable.
4. Put an A for achievement when it was because you accomplished something you had wanted to.
5. After doing this for a week can you reorganise your days to include more P's? Can you put some more P's before A's, pleasure before business?

Aim to find the positive influences in your life.

Differentiate between positive and negative experiences.

This may seem time-consuming, but aren't you worth the effort? It will help you regain an understanding and appreciation of what you enjoy. At times when we have been knocked off our path we need to do something more planned and systematic rather than just hoping that things will get better.

Example

TIME	MON	TUES	WED	THURS	FRI	SAT	SUN
8:00	Drove to school listening to Bach = 7						
9:00	Took register, 3 absent = 8						
10:00	Meeting with parent = 4						
11:00	Break - colleagues = 5						
12:00	Confrontation with two students = 3						

Positive thinking

1. One thing I like about myself is

....

2. One of my best lessons is

....

3. Something I do very well is

....

4. A difficulty I handled well recently was

....

5. My pupils always like it when I

....

6. An example of me caring for others is

....

7. My school colleagues can always count on me to

....

8. One goal I'm presently working on is

....

9. One important thing I intend doing in the next two months is

....

10. One way in which I am very dependable is

....

11. They say I did a good job when I

....

12. One of my best qualities is

....

13. Something I can handle better now is

....

14. I pleasantly surprised myself when I

....

15. When I'm at my best I

....

16. A value that I try hard to practise is

....

17. I think I have the strength to

....

18. A skill I'm proud to possess is

....

19. One thing I've overcome is

....

20. If I had to say just one good thing about myself it would be

....

21. A compliment that I was recently paid was

....

22. I really helped a parent when I

....

23. A good example of my ability to manage life is

....

24. A time when I was really able to help a pupil was

....

25. I often help other people through·

....

26. When I think of how I've changed I'm really proud that I

....

27. One way in which I successfully controlled my emotions was

....

Mind Markers
Remember the need we have to place signs in our mind to warn us of
DANGER. Perhaps there is a "hair pin" bend ahead, or perhaps we have
entered some marshy area. Without warning signs we would get into worse
trouble. Sometimes just a picture or even a sound could be warning
enough. Without such warnings many of us are in danger of driving "off
the edge". Here is an example of a paranoid thought. "I am worried that
you will leave me." I keep checking on your whereabouts. I question you
aggressively. I go through your personal belongings. (All of these
actions feed and strengthen the paranoid thought.) Being paranoid I
ignore all evidence that shows you are open, honest, trustworthy and
caring. What happens? In the end you leave me because I am so untrusting,
etc. Which is what my paranoia thought would happen anyway. WE
MUST learn to recognise such irrational thought processes AND TAKE
ACTION.

Here are some of my key Mind Markers.

Life is difficult
There are many challenges in life, no one has a problem-free existence.

20

Zig Zag
If you are at A and you want to get to B you may need to go through C, D and E.

Know the solution
Be solution focused. Break the solution down into small steps.

Is this a problem or an inconvenience?
When you break your back or your house burns down, then you have a problem. Most other challenges do not justify an "over the top" reaction.

If it helps use it, if not leave it
Support is always being offered; we are not always ready to take it. Be prepared to take help when offered and leave the rest alone.

Recognise the voices from the past
Don't be pulled by unhelpful strings from your past.

Happiness ensues from what you do
You have as much right to be happy as anyone. Happiness is not something you have to earn. But you cannot pursue happiness. It results from what you do.

You are more than what you think, feel and do
You can learn to take control of your thoughts and actions and this will affect what you feel. You can take control.

Change is inevitable
Nothing lasts for ever. Make sure you take the time to enjoy where you are as much as planning where you are going. Otherwise life will happen while you are planning what you are going to do.

Each day will be a challenge in some way or other. You can just wait and hope that it is reasonable or you can try to make it positive. Imagine you had a skin disorder. Your G.P. has prescribed a course of treatment. Each day you have to take certain vitamins and use a specific ointment. You wouldn't question whether or not you should use the treatments. Would you? Well, what we are aiming for are mental health vitamins. Things that you need to do each day to help you cope with the pressures you face.

A Minimalist's Survival Guide

Each day:

Exercise
for at least 20 minutes.
Recognise good news
record good events.
Have some humour
smiling is an antidote to stress.
Set goals
Small, Measurable, Achievable, Realistic, Timed.
Treat yourself
have a range of treats and activities.

Managing time

How do you respond to pressure? Each day we have a set amount of time.
A day is only 24 hours, no more no less. There is no more time available
than what you have.

Time is life

To manage time is to manage your life.
To waste time is to waste your life.

We can divide our time up into four areas. We all need some of the following
activities:

1. ACTIVITY TIME – to exercise our body
2. SOCIAL TIME – to be with friends
3. NOTHING TIME – to switch off
4. PERSONAL TIME – to reflect

In the figure on the next page you can work out a daily programme for
yourself. (Some activities could be in several categories.) Choose at least
two from each and place them into the circle. Now because we all differ in
how we respond to pressure, we each need more of some of those activities
than others. Write at least two more in the areas that apply to you.

DO YOU get very angry when under pressure? Do you worry about
exploding and acting aggressively? IF YOU DO then make sure you do
more active physical activities.

DO YOU become physically exhausted, head-achey, tense muscles etc? IF YOU DO explore ways of relaxing, aromatherapy, reflexology, yoga - spend more time in hot, bubbly baths.

DO YOU become cynical and negative? IF YOU DO spend more time with people who uplift you, read, watch films that inspire you. Remember why you became a teacher.

DO YOU feel confused about the direction of your life and question your value? If you do, you may well be in a "life-crisis". Use your questions to explore alternatives, meet like-minded people, use your questions to achieve deeper insight, understanding and spiritual awareness.

PERSONAL EFFECTIVENESS

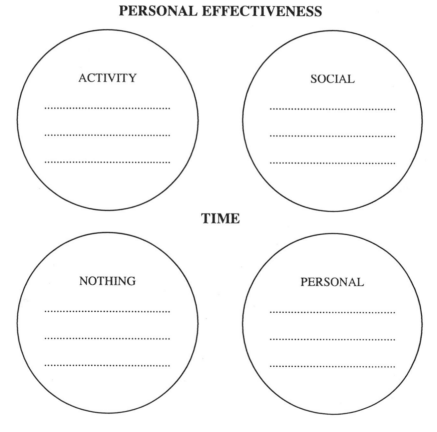

ACTIVITY

....

....

....

SOCIAL

....

....

....

TIME

NOTHING

....

....

....

PERSONAL

....

....

....

References

Butler, G. & Hope, T. (1995) *Manage Your Mind, the mental fitness guide,* Oxford University Press: Oxford.

Fulghum, R. (1989) *All I really need to know I learned in kindergarten,* Grafton Books: London.

Holland, S. & Ward, C. (1990) *Assertiveness: A practical approach,* Winslow Press: Bicester.

Kopp, S. (1993) *If You Meet the Buddha on the Road, Kill Him!* Sheldon Press: London.

Millman, D. (1984) *Way of the Peaceful Warrior,* Krammer Inc.: Tiburon, CA.

Powell, T. (1992) *The Mental Health Handbook,* Winslow Press: Bicester.

Roger, J. & McWilliams, P. (1991) *Life 101 Everything we wish we had learned about life in school - but didn't,* Prelude Press: Los Angeles, CA.

Simmons, M. & Daw, P. (1994) *Stress, Anxiety, Depression: a practical workbook,* Winslow Press: Bicester.

Yalom, I. (1989) *Love's Executioner,* Penguin: London.